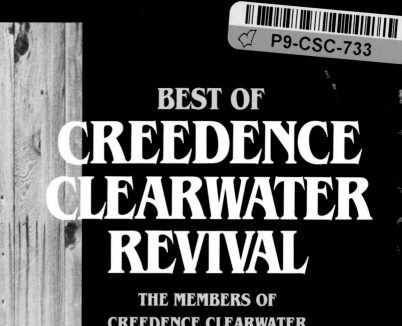

BEST OF
CREEDENCE CLEARWATER REVIVAL

THE MEMBERS OF CREEDENCE CLEARWATER REVIVAL ARE:
DOUG CLIFFORD
STUART COOK
JOHN FOGERTY
TOM FOGERTY

© 1989 CPP/Belwin, Inc.
15800 N.W. 48th Avenue, Miami, Forida 33014
Design: Frank Milone
ISBN: 0-89898-454-8

GREEN RIVER

J.C. FOGERTY

Well, take me back down where cool wat-er flows,

Let me re-mem-ber things I love, Stop-pin' at the log where

cat-fish bite, Walk-in' a-long the riv-er road at night, Bare-foot girls

Green River - 3 - 1

6

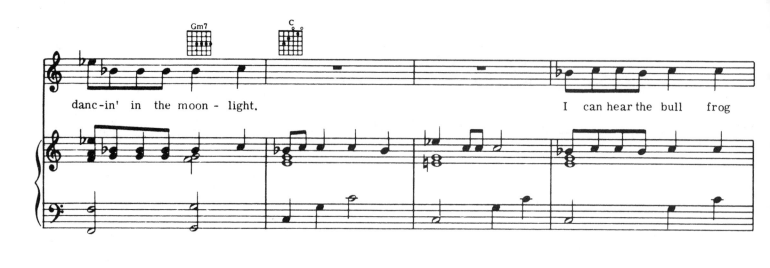

Riv-er._____ Up at Co-dy's camp I spent my days

With flat car rid-ers and cross_____ tie walk-ers.

Old Co - dy, Jun - ior took me o - ver. Said,"You're gon - na find the world_

_ is smoul - d'rin'. If you get lost come on home_ to Green Riv-er."_____

BAD MOON RISING

J.C. FOGERTY

I see the bad moon a-ris-ing.
I hear hur-ri-canes a-blow-ing.
Hope you got your things to-geth-er.

I see trou-ble on the way.
I know the end is com-ing soon.
Hope you are quite pre-pared to die.

I see earth-quakes and light-nin'.
I fear riv-ers ov-er flow-ing.
Looks like we're in for nas-ty weath-er.

Bad Moon Rising - 2 - 1

I see bad times to - day.
I hear the voice of rage and ruin.
One eye is tak - en for an eye.

Don't go a - round to - night, Well, it's bound to take your life,

1. 2.

There's a bad moon on the rise. *To Coda* ⊕

3. *D.S. al* ⊕ *Coda*

⊕ *Coda* rise.

TEARIN' UP THE COUNTRY

D. CLIFFORD

Brightly

1. Play - in' a pa - vil - ion on the out - skirts of town,
2. Mom and pa - pa told me "Son, you got - ta go to school;
3. Ran in - to a dry spell,_____ seemed no - where to go.

Play - in' where my roll - er der - by rolls. Just a
On - ly way to make the fam - 'ly proud." I re-
Good luck turned the tide, I'm on my way. You

part - time mu - sic man, A no - bod - y at the plant, I'm
I paid no at - ten - tion, left my books at home, You
mem - ber load - in' big trucks when the sum - mer sun was hot,

Tearin' Up The Country - 3 - 1

Tear - in' Up The Coun - try with a song.

Rath - er play my mu - sic real loud._____
know I could still be there, but I'm not._____

1.
2. Tear-in' Up The Coun - try with a song._____

3.
4. Tear-in' Up The Coun - try with a song._____ I'm

Tear-in' up the coun - try with a song.
Tear-in' up the coun - try with a song.

Tearin' Up The Country - 3 - 3

DOOR TO DOOR

S. COOK

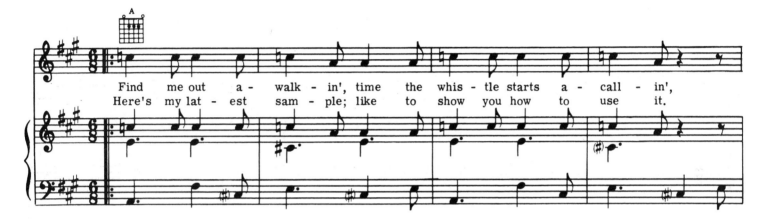

Find me out a - walk - in', time the whis - tle starts a - call - in',
Here's my lat - est sam - ple; like to show you how to use it.

May - be stop - pin' ear - ly, knock - in' at your___ door.___ Take so long to
First, you pull the cur - tain while I spread some___ here.___ Wipe the sur - face

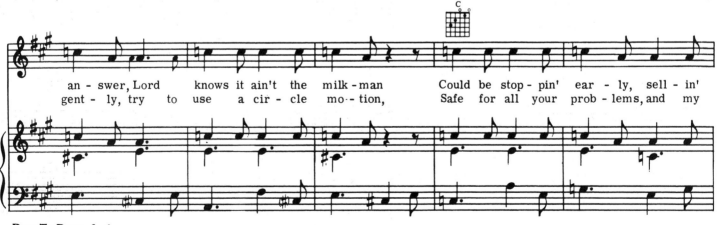

an - swer, Lord knows it ain't the milk - man, Could be stop - pin' ear - ly, sell - in'
gent - ly, try to use a cir - cle mo - tion, Safe for all your prob - lems, and my

Door To Door - 3 - 1

14

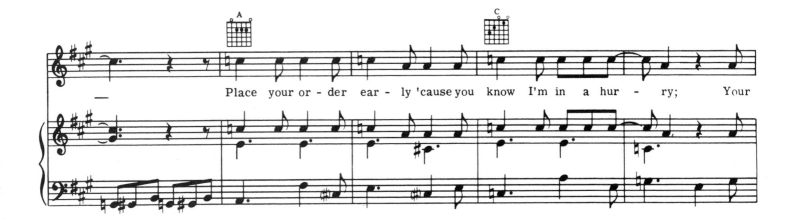

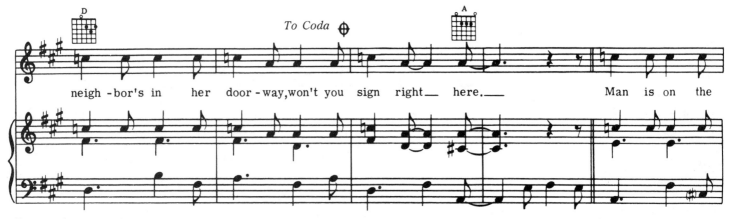

Door To Door - 3 - 2

LODI

J.C. FOGERTY

Lodi - 2 - 1

HEY, TONIGHT

J.C. FOGERTY

Moderately

Hey, To-night,____ Gon-na be__ to-night,____

Don't you know__ I'm fly - in' To - night,____ to-

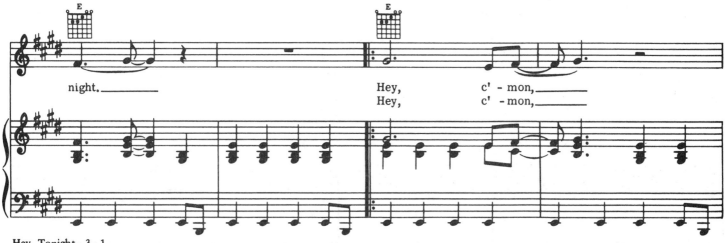

night._____ Hey, c' - mon,____
Hey, c' - mon,____

Hey, Tonight - 3 - 1

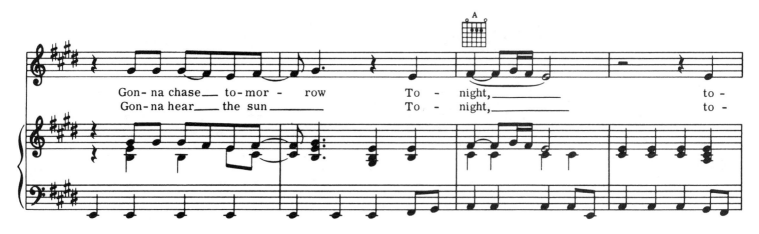

Gon-na chase__ to-mor - row To - night,_____ to-
Gon-na hear__ the sun_____ To - night,_____ to-

night._____
night._____

Gon-na get it to the raft - ers,

Watch me now. Jo-dy's gon-na get re - li - gion

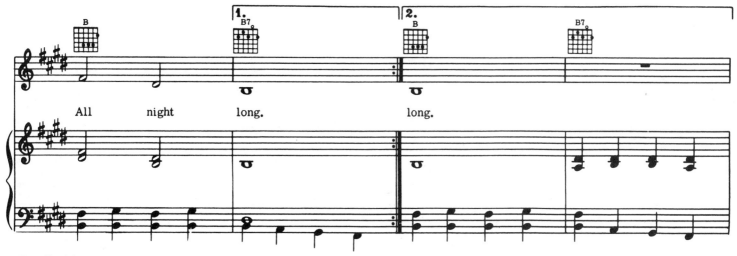

All night long. long.

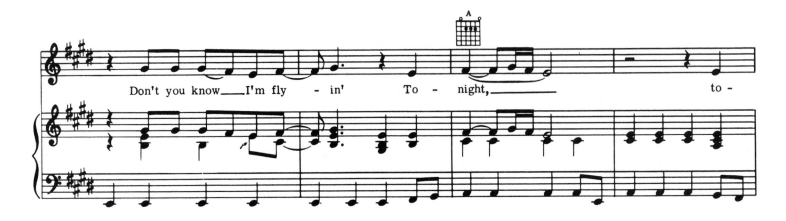

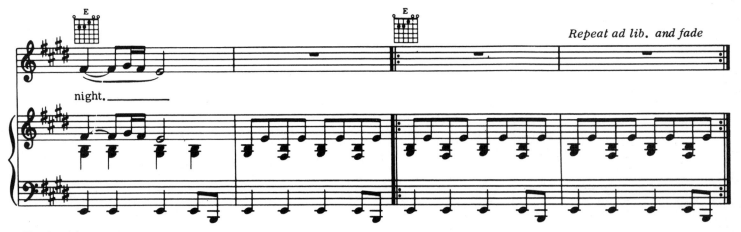

Hey, Tonight - 3 - 3

THE MIDNIGHT SPECIAL

J.C. FOGERTY

The Midnight Special - 3 - 2

ap-ron_____ And the clothes she___ wore. Um-b'rel-la on her
gam-ble,_____ There, you bet-ter not___ fight, Or the sher-iff will

shoul-der _____ Piece of pa-per in her hand; She come to see the
grab ya _____ And the boys will bring you down. The next thing you

gov-'nor_____ She wants to free her___ man. Let the Mid-night
know, boy,_____ Oh! you're pri-son___ bound._____

1.

2. *D.S. al ◆ Coda*

Well, let the Mid-night

Coda

ev-er-lov-in' light___ on me._____

The Midnight Special - 3 - 3

SWEET HITCH-HIKER

J.C. FOGERTY

Moderately Bright (in 4)

VERSE

1. Was Rid-in' a-long-side the high-way,— ——— Roll-in' up the coun-try-side.
2. (Cruis)—— in' on thru the junc-tion,— I'm—— fly-in' 'bout the speed of sound,
3. (Was) bust-ed up a long the high-way,— I'm the sad-dest rid-in' fool a-live.

Think-in' I'm the de-vil's heat-wave,— What you burn in your cra——zy mind?——
No—— tic-in' pe-cu-liar func-tion,— Cain't no rol-ler coast-er—— show me down,
Won-d'ring if you're go-in' my—— way,— Won't you give a poor—— boy a ride?——

—————— Saw a slight dis-trac-tion— Stand-in' by the road;—
—————— I turned a-way to see—— her,— Woa! she caught my eye,—
—————— Here she comes a-rid-in'— Lord, she's fly-in' high.—

Sweet Hitch-Hiker - 2 - 1

Sweet Hitch-Hiker - 2 - 2

BORN ON THE BAYOU

J.C. FOGERTY

Moderately

VERSE 1 F7

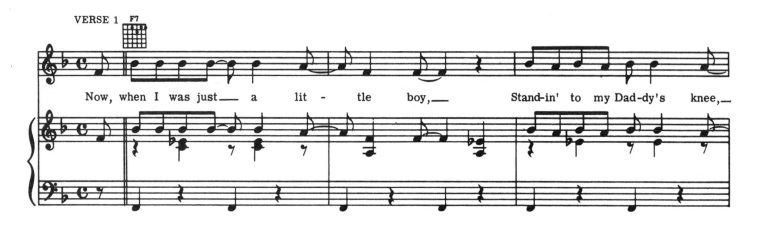

Now, when I was just a lit - tle boy, Stand-in' to my Dad-dy's knee,

My pop-pa said, "Son, don't let the man get you and do what he done to me."

Born On The Bayou - 3 - 1

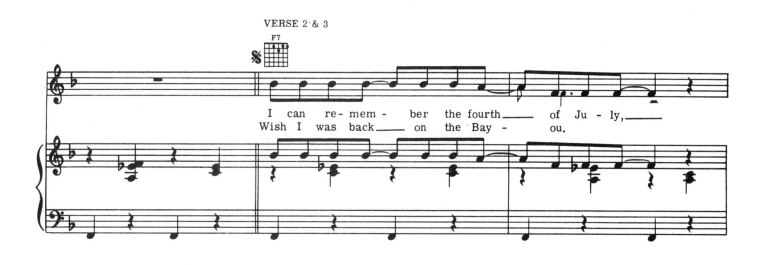

Born On The Bayou - 3 - 2

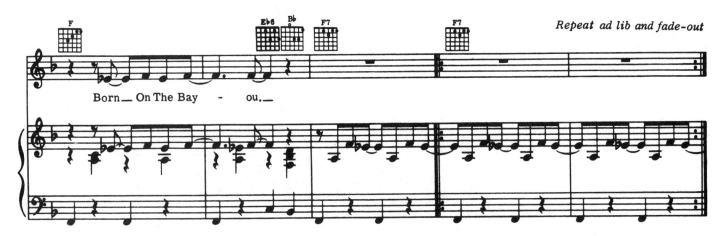

TRAVELIN' BAND

J.C. FOGERTY

Travelin' Band - 3 - 1

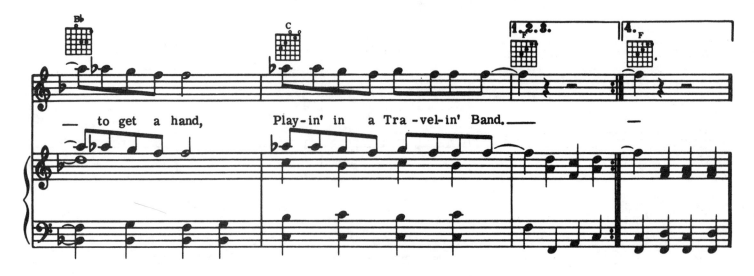

to get a hand, Play-in' in a Tra-vel-in' Band.____ —

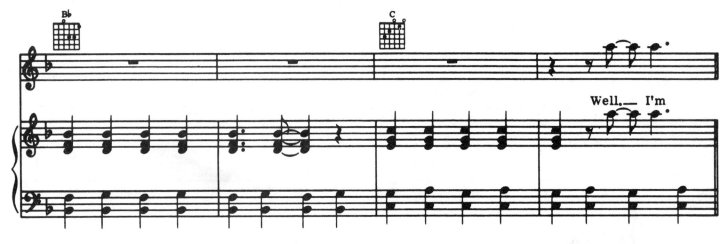

Well,____ I'm

play-in' in a Tra-vel-in' Band;____ Play-in' in a Trav-el-in' Band.____

Travelin' Band - 3 - 3

FORTUNATE SON

J.C. FOGERTY

Moderately bright (in Four)

VERSE

Some folks are born made to wave the flag,
Some folks are born sil - ver spoon in hand,
Some folks in - her - it star span - gled eyes,

Ooh, they're red, white and blue. And when the band plays
Lord, don't they help them - selves. But when the tax man
Ooh, they send you down to war. And when you ask them,

"Hail to the chief", They point the can-non right at you.
comes to the door, Lord, the house looks like a rum-mage sale.
"How much should we give?" _____ They on - ly ans - wer More! more! more!

Fortunate Son - 2 - 1

LOOKIN' OUT MY BACK DOOR

J.C. FOGERTY

Moderately Fast

Just got home from Il - li - nois, lock the front door, oh boy!
gi - ant do - ing cart-wheels, a stat - ue wear - in' high heels.
For - ward trou - bles Il - li - nois, lock the front door, oh boy!

Got to sit down, take a rest on the porch. I -
Look at all the hap - py crea - tures danc - ing on the lawn.
Look at all the hap - py crea - tures danc - ing on the lawn.

mag - in - a - tion sets in, pret - ty soon I'm sing - in',
di - no - saur Vic - tro - la list - 'ning to Buck O - wens. Doo, doo,
Both - er me to - mor - row, to - day I'll buy no sor - rows.

Lookin' Out My Back Door - 2 - 1

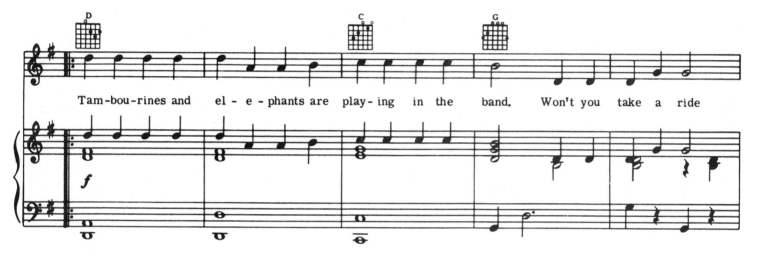

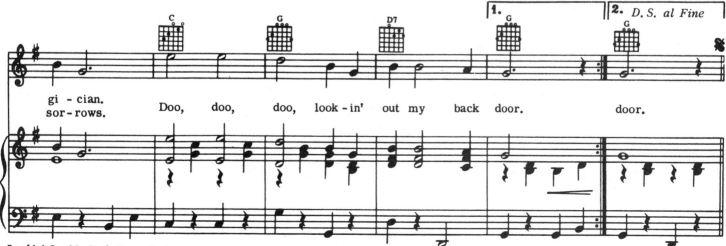

Lookin' Out My Back Door - 2 - 2

DOWN ON THE CORNER

J.C. FOGERTY

Down On The Corner - 2 - 1

SUSIE-Q

Words and Music by
D. HAWKINS, S.J. LEWIS
and E. BROADWATER

Suzie - Q - 2 - 1

PROUD MARY

J.C. FOGERTY

Proud Mary - 2 - 1

To Coda ⊕

in',___ roll - in',___ roll - in' on the riv - er.___

VERSE

If you come down___ to the riv - er, Bet you gon-na find some peo - ple who live.___

D. S. al ⊕ Coda 𝄌

You don't have to wor- ry___ 'cause you have no mon-ey,___ Peo-ple on the riv-er are hap-py to give.___

⊕ *Coda*

Repeat ad lib and fade out

Roll-in',___ roll - in',___ roll-in' on the riv - er.___

Proud Mary - 2 - 2

HAVE YOU EVER SEEN THE RAIN?

J.C. FOGERTY

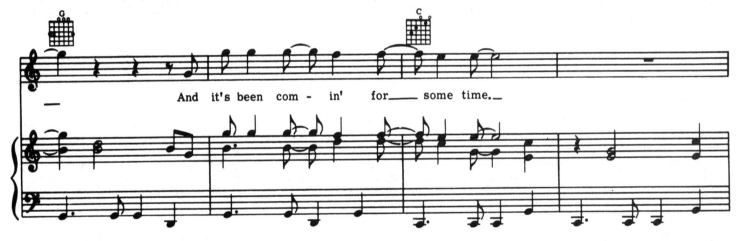

Have You Ever Seen The Rain? - 3 - 1

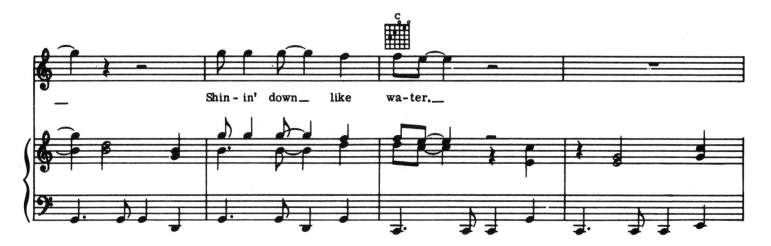

Shin - in' down__ like wa-ter.__

CHORUS

I want to know,_____ Have you ev - er__ seen the rain?

I want to know,_____ Have you ev - er__ seen the rain

To Coda

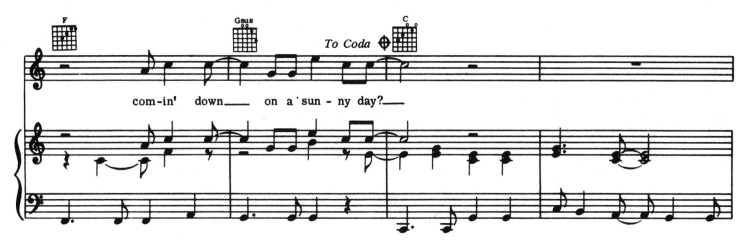

com-in' down__ on a `sun - ny day?__

WHO'LL STOP THE RAIN

J.C. FOGERTY

Who'll Stop The Rain - 3 - 1

46

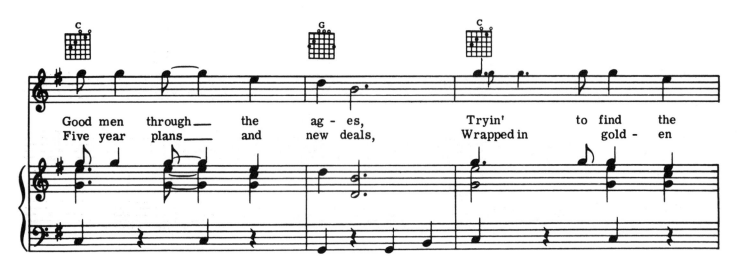

Good men through the ag - es,
Five year plans and new deals,
Tryin' to find the
Wrapped in gold - en

sun;
chains.
And I won - der, Still I won - der, Who'll Stop The Rain.

Heard the sing - ers play - in', How we cheered for more. The

Who'll Stop The Rain - 3 - 2

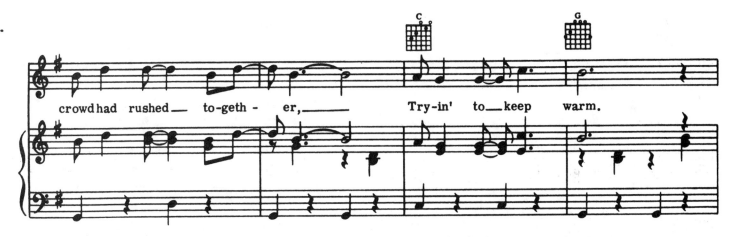

crowd had rushed to-geth - er,_____ Try-in' to_keep warm.

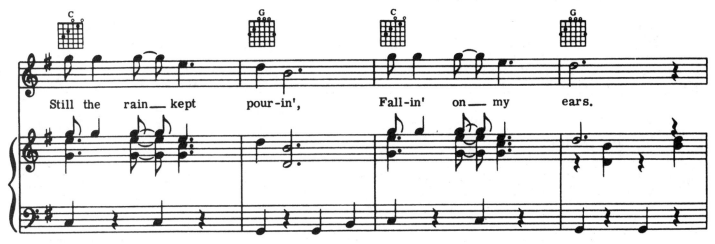

Still the rain_kept pour-in', Fall-in' on_my ears.

And I won-der, Still I won-der, Who'll Stop The Rain._____

Repeat and fade

Who'll Stop The Rain - 3 - 3

WALK ON THE WATER

Words and Music by
TOM FOGERTY and
J.C. FOGERTY

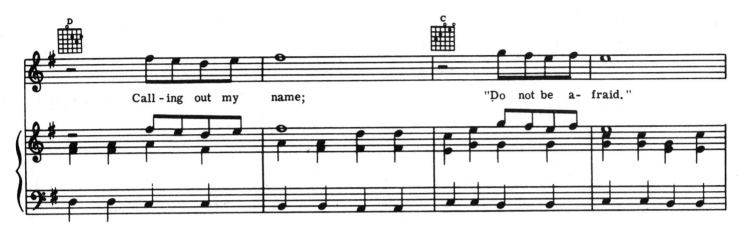

Call-ing out my name; "Do not be a-fraid."

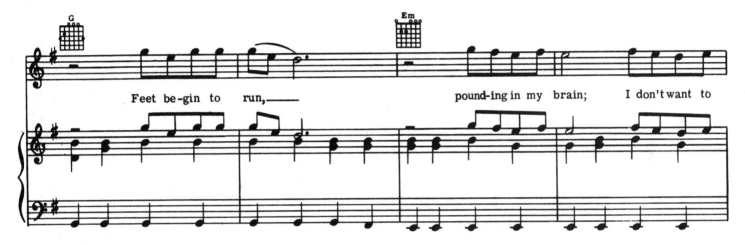

Feet be-gin to run,_____ pound-ing in my brain; I don't want to

go;_____ I don't want to go. No, no, no,

no, a-no._____ I don't want to go.

BORN ON THE BAYOU

J.C. FOGERTY

Now, when I was just ___ a lit - tle boy, ___ stand - in' to my Dad - dy's knee, ___ my

pop - pa said, "Son, don't let ___ the man get you and do ___ what he done to me."

chas - in' down a hoo-doo there, ___ chas - in' down a hoo-doo there. ___

___ choog - lin' on down to New Or - leans. ___ Born ___ on the Bay - ou;

born ___ on the Bay - ou; ___ born ___ on the Bay - ou.

Verse 2:
I can remember the Fourth of July,
Runnin' through the backwood, bare.
And I can still hear my old hound dog barkin',
Chasin' down a hoodoo there,
Chasin' down a hoodoo there. *(To Chorus:)*

Verse 3:
Wish I was back on the Bayou,
Rollin' with some Cajun Queen.
Wishin' I were a fast freight train,
Just a chooglin' on down to New Orleans. *(To Chorus:)*

GREEN RIVER

J.C. FOGERTY

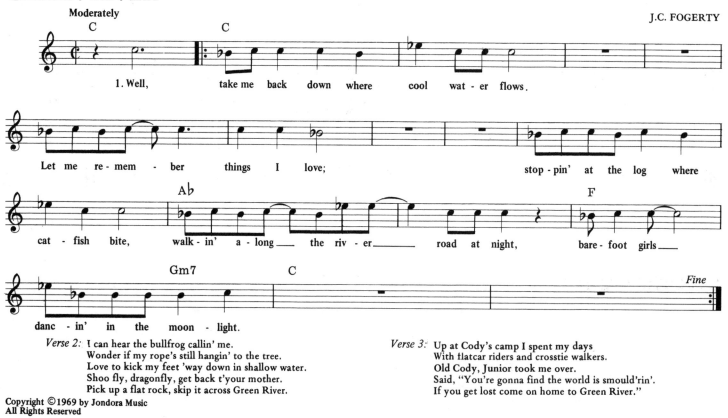

1. Well, take me back down where cool wat - er flows.

Let me re - mem - ber things I love; stop - pin' at the log where

cat - fish bite, walk - in' a - long ___ the riv - er ___ road at night, bare - foot girls ___

danc - in' in the moon - light.

Verse 2: I can hear the bullfrog callin' me.
Wonder if my rope's still hangin' to the tree.
Love to kick my feet 'way down in shallow water.
Shoo fly, dragonfly, get back t'your mother.
Pick up a flat rock, skip it across Green River.

Verse 3: Up at Cody's camp I spent my days
With flatcar riders and crosstie walkers.
Old Cody, Junior took me over.
Said, "You're gonna find the world is smould'rin'.
If you get lost come on home to Green River."

TEARIN' UP THE COUNTRY

D. CLIFFORD

DOOR TO DOOR

S. COOK

Brightly

Verse: A

1. Find me out a-walk-in', time the whis-tle starts a-call-in',

C / D7 / A

may-be stop-pin' ear-ly, knock-in' at your door. Take so long to

C

an-swer, Lord knows it ain't the milk-man. Could be stop-pin' ear-ly, sell-in'

D / 1. A / 2.3. A / *Chorus:* E

door to door. This stuff 'll get the stain out if you

use it loose-ly wad-ded; this here 'll take the pain out and won't

A

mess your hair. Place your or-der ear-ly 'cause you

C / D7

know I'm in a hur-ry; your neigh-bor's in her door-way, won't you

1. A / *D.C.* 2. / *Repeat ad lib. and fade*

sign right here? sign right here?

Verse 2:
Here's my latest sample; like to show you how to use it.
First, you pull the curtain while I spread some here.
Wipe the surface gently, try to use a circle motion;
Safe for all your problems and my price is fair. *(To Chorus:)*

Verse 3:
Man is on the last train, all that work and no play;
Could be stoppin' early, knockin' at your door.
Time for me to head on; pack my kit and 'So long;'
Catch you bright and early sellin' door to door. *(To Chorus:)*

SUSIE-Q

Words and Music by
D. HAWKINS, S.J. LEWIS
and E. BROADWATER

Oh, Susie Q, Oh, Susie Q, Oh, Susie Q, how I love you, my Susie Q.

Verse:
1. I like the way you walk
2. Well, say that you'll be true,

I like the way you talk;
Well, say that you'll be true;

I like the way you walk, I like the way you
Well, say that you'll be true and never leave me

talk, my Susie Q.
blue, my Susie Q.

2. Oh, Susie Q.

LODI

J.C. FOGERTY

Moderately

1. Just about a year ago I set out on the road,

seekin' my fame and fortune, lookin' for a pot of gold. Things got bad, and

things got worse, I guess you will know the tune. Oh, Lord! Stuck in Lodi a-

gain. Oh, Lord! I'm stuck in Lodi again.

Verse 2:
Rode in on the Greyhound, I'll be walkin' out if I go.
I was just passin' through; must be seven months or more.
Ran out of time and money; looks like they took my friends.
Oh, Lord! I'm stuck in Lodi again.

Verse 3:
The man from the magazine said I was on my way.
Somewhere I lost connections, ran out of songs to play.
I came into town, a one-night stand; looks like my plans fell through.
Oh, Lord! Stuck in Lodi again.

Verse 4:
If I only had a dollar for every song I've sung,
And ev'ry time I've had to play while people sat there drunk,
You know, I'd catch the next train back to where I live.
Oh, Lord! I'm stuck in Lodi again.
Oh, Lord! I'm stuck in Lodi again.

HEY, TONIGHT

J.C. FOGERTY

THE MIDNIGHT SPECIAL

J.C. FOGERTY

Moderately

1. Well, you wake up in the morn-in', you hear the work bell ring, and they march you to the ta-ble to see the same old thing. Ain't no food up-on the ta-ble, and no fork up in the pan. But you bet-ter not com-plain, boy, you get in trou-ble with the man.

Chorus: Let the Mid-night Spec-cial shine a light on me, let the Mid-night Spe-cial shine a light on me. let the Mid-night Spe-cial shine a light on me, let the Mid-night Spe-cial shine a ev-er-lov-in' light on me.

2. Yon-der come Miss Ros-
3. If you're ev-er in Hous-

light on me.

*1st verse tempo rubato (to chorus)

Verse 2:
Yonder come Miss Rosie,
How in the world did you know?
By the way she wears her apron
And the clothes she wore.
Umbrella on her shoulder,
Piece of paper in her hand;
She come to see the gov'nor:
She wants to free her man.
(To Chorus:)

Verse 3:
If you're ever in Houston,
Well, you better do right;
You better not gamble,
There, you better not fight,
Or the sheriff will grab ya
And the boys will bring you down.
The next thing you know, boy,
Oh! You're prison bound.
(To Chorus:)

SWEET HITCH-HIKER

Moderately bright

J.C. FOGERTY

1. Was rid-in' a-long-side the high-way, roll-in' up the coun-ty-side; think-in' I'm the De-vil's heat-wave, what you burn in your cra-zy mind?

Saw a slight dis-trac-tion stand-in' by the road; she was smil-in' there, yel-low in her hair; do you wan-na, I was think-in' would you care?

Chorus:

Sweet hitch-(a)-hik-er, we could make mu-sic at the Greas-y King.

Sweet hitch-(a)-hik-er, won't you ride on my fast ma-chine?

2. Cruis- ma-chine?
3. Was

Verse 2:
Cruisin' on thru the junction,
I'm flyin' 'bout the speed of sound,
Noticin' peculiar function,
Can't no roller coaster slow me down.
I turned away to see her,
Woa! She caught my eye,
But I was rollin' down, movin' too fast;
Do you wanna, she was thinkin', can it last?
(To Chorus:)

Verse 3:
Was busted up along the highway,
I'm the saddest ridin' fool alive.
Wond'ring if you're goin' my way,
Won't you give a poor boy a ride?
Here she comes a-ridin';
Lord, she's flyin' high.
But she was rollin' down, movin' too fast;
Do you wanna, she was thinkin', can I last?
(To Chorus:)

TRAVELIN' BAND

J.C. FOGERTY

Fairly bright

Verse:
1. Sev-en-thir-ty-sev-en com-in' out of the sky.___ Won't you take me down to Mem-phis on a mid-night ride. I wan-na move. Play-in' in a trav-el-in' band.___ Yeah!___

Well, I'm fly-in' 'cross the land, tryin'___ to get a hand, play-in' in a trav-el-in' band.___

Well,___ I'm play-in' in a trav-el-in' band.___

Play-in' in a trav-el-in' band.___ Play-in' in a trav-el-in' band.___ Well, I'm play-in' in a trav-el-in' band.___

Well, I'm fly-in' 'cross the land, tryin'___ to get a hand, play-in' in a trav-el-in' band.___

Verse 2:
Take me to the hotel; baggage gone, oh, well.
Come on, come on, won't you get me to my room,
I wanna move . . .

Verse 3:
Listen to the radio, talkin' 'bout the last show.
Someone got excited, had to call the State Militia;
Wanna move . . .

Verse 4:
Here we come again on a Saturday night
With your fussin' and a fightin' - won't you get me to the rhyme,
I wanna move . . .

58

FORTUNATE SON

J.C. FOGERTY

1. Some folks are born made to wave the flag; ooh, they're red, white and blue.
2. Some folks are born, sil - ver spoon in hand; Lord, don't they help them - selves.
3. Some folks in - her - it star - span-gled eyes; ooh, they send you down to war.

And when the band plays "Hail To The Chief", they point the can -non right at you.
But when the tax man comes to the door, Lord, the house looks like a rum-mage sale.
And when you ask them "How much should we give?", they on - ly ans-wer more! more! more!

It ain't me, it ain't me __ I ain't no { sen - a - tor's / mil-lion-aire's / mil - i - ta - ry } son. It ain't me,

it ain't me; __ I ain't no for - tun-ate one. one. one.

WHO'LL STOP THE RAIN

J.C. FOGERTY

1. Long as I __ re - mem - ber, the rain been com-in' down.

Clouds of mys - ter pour - in' con - fu - sion on the ground. __ Good men through _ the ag - es,

tryin' to find the sun; and I won - der, still I won - der, who'll stop the rain. __

Verse 2:
I went down Virginia, seekin' shelter from the storm.
Caught up in the fable, I watched the tower grow.
Five-year plans and new deals, wrapped in golden chains.
And I wonder, still I wonder, who'll stop the rain.

Verse 3:
Heard the singers playin', how we cheered for more.
The crowd had rushed together, tryin' to keep warm.
Still the rain kept pourin', fallin' on my ears.
And I wonder, still I wonder, who'll stop the rain.

LOOKIN' OUT MY BACK DOOR

J.C. FOGERTY

DOWN ON THE CORNER

J.C. FOGERTY

PROUD MARY

J.C. FOGERTY

Moderately *(with a heavy beat)*

1. Left a good job___ in the cit - y, work - in' for the man ev - 'ry night and day, ___

and I nev - er lost one min - ute of sleep - in', wor - ry - in' 'bout the way things might have been.___

Chorus:

Big wheel keep on turn - in', Proud Mar - y keep on burn - in', Roll -

- in', roll - in', roll - in' on the riv - er._____ Roll -

Verse 2:
Cleaned a lot of plates in Memphis,
Pumped a lot of pain in New Orleans,
But I never saw the good side of the city,
Until I hitched a ride on a river boat queen.
(To Chorus:)

Verse 3:
If you come down to the river,
Bet you gonna find some people who live.
You don't have to worry 'cause you have no money,
People on the river are happy to give.
(To Chorus:)

BAD MOON RISING

J.C. FOGERTY

HAVE YOU EVER SEEN THE RAIN?

J.C. FOGERTY

Verse 3: Yesterday, and days before,
Sun is cold and rain is hard, I know;
Been that way for all my time.

Verse 4: 'Til forever, on it goes
Through the circle, fast and slow, I know;
And it can't stop, I wonder.
(To Chorus:)

WALK ON THE WATER

Words and Music by
TOM FOGERTY and
J.C. FOGERTY

SUPERSTARS OF AMERICAN POP

BEST OF CREEDENCE CLEARWATER REVIVAL
___ (P0700SMX)

This piano/vocal/chords edition features 18 of Creedence Clearwater Revival's greatest songs. Fake arrangements of each tune are provided also. Contents include: Bad Moon Rising ● Proud Mary ● Have You Ever ● Who'll Stop The Rain ● Born On The Bayou and more.

CREEDENCE CLEARWATER REVIVAL / COMPLETE
___ (P0408SMX)

Arranged for piano/vocal/chords, this collection contains 65 songs. Contents include: I Put A Spell On You ● Suzie Q ● Born On The Bayou ● Proud Mary ● Green River ● Bad Moon Rising ● Lodi ● Down On The Corner ● Fortunate Son ● Who'll Stop The Rain ● Travelin' Band ● Lookin' Out My Back Door ● Have You Ever Seen The Rain? ● Hey, Tonight ● Sweet Hitch-Hiker and many more.

THE DOORS COMPLETE
___ (P0443SMX)

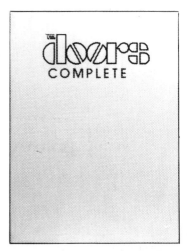

The Doors: the legendary group of the late 60's who helped usher in the era of self-awareness. Mystical Jim Morrison captured the imagination of America's youth. This piano/vocal/chords folio recaptures it all with great music including: The Crystal Ship ● L.A. Woman ● Break On Through ● Riders On The Storm ● Runnin' Blues ● The Soft Parade ● Touch Me and Wishful Sinful.

THE DOORS GREATEST HITS
___ (P0442SMX)

Arranged for piano/vocal/chords, this matching songbook features the same great songs recorded on the album. Rekindle the memories with ten of The Doors biggest hits, including: Light My Fire ● Hello, I Love You ● People Are Strange ● Love Me Two Times and more.

BEST OF THE BEACH BOYS
___ (P0675SMX)

Enjoy these ever-popular songs made famous by The Beach Boys. This piano/vocal/chords collection includes 18 top hits such as: Help Me Rhonda ● California Girls ● Fun, Fun, Fun ● I Get Around ● Surfer Girl ● Wouldn't It Be Nice and more. Join in the fun!

THE BEST OF THE BEACH BOYS
PIANO/VOCAL/CHORDS

All Summer Long	Fun, Fun, Fun	Little Deuce Coupe
	Getcha Back	Shut Down
Barbara Ann	Girls On The Beach	Surfer Girl
California Girls	Help Me Rhonda	Surfin'
		Surfin' Safari
Catch A Wave	I Get Around	Surfin' U.S.A.
Do It Again	In My Room	Wouldn't It Be Nice
409		

THE BEACH BOYS COMPLETE — Vol. 1
___ (P0413SMX)

Over 70 songs made famous by The Beach Boys! Arranged for piano/vocal/chords, the songs include: Help Me Rhonda ● Surfin' Safari ● Little Deuce Coupe ● California Girls ● Barbara Ann ● I Get Around ● Wendy ● Don't Worry Baby ● Wouldn't It Be Nice ● Fun, Fun, Fun ● In My Room ● When I Grow Up (To Be A Man) ● 409 ● All Summer Long and more!

THE BEST OF THE FOUR TOPS
___ (P0774SMX)

In this successful "Best Of" Series, enjoy memorable songs from the 60's! The sixteen titles include: Baby I Need Your Loving ● Bernadette ● I Can't Help Myself (Sugar Pie, Honey Bunch) ● It's The Same Old Song ● 7 Rooms Of Gloom ● Shake Me ● Wake Me (When It's Over).

THE BEST OF THE FOUR TOPS
PIANO/VOCAL/CHORDS

Ask The Lonely	Loving You Is Sweeter Than Ever	Standing In The Shadows Of Love
Baby I Need Your Loving	Reach Out I'll Be There	Still Water (Love)
Bernadette	7 Rooms	What Is A Man?

THE BEST OF THE SUPREMES
___ (P0771SMX)

These songs live on through the decades! Play and sing such timeless hits as Baby Love ● Come See About Me ● I Hear A Symphony ● My World Is Empty Without You ● Stop! In The Name Of Love ● Someday We'll Be Together ● You Can't Hurry Love and Love Child.

THE BEST OF THE SUPREMES
PIANO/VOCAL/CHORDS

Baby Love	Love Child	Reflections
Back In My Arms Again	Love Is Here And Now You're Gone	Someday We'll Be Together
Come See About Me	My World Is Empty Without You	Stop! In The Name Of Love
The Happening		You Can't Hurry Love
I Hear A Symphony	Nothing But Heartaches	You Keep Me Hangin' On
In And Out Of Love		

THE BEST OF THE TEMPTATIONS
___ (P0772SMX)

Contains these hit songs: Ain't Too Proud To Beg ● Cloud Nine ● Get Ready ● Just My Imagination (Running Away With Me) ● My Girl and Papa Was A Rolling Stone.